PALESTINE

Prophetic Principles
Over Prophecies

Louay M. Safi

Visionary Leaders
Indianapolis, IN

Palestine
Prophetic Principles Over Prophecies
All Rights Reserved.
Copyright © 2009, 2011 Louay Safi
V.1. R.2

ISBN: 978-1460949917 (paperback)

PRINTED IN THE UNITED STATES OF AMERICA

To the free spirits
whose deep faith
in the power of Justice
has sustained them through
sixty years of pain and suffering
without ever losing confidence
in the inevitable triumph
of right over might
and hope in a rewarding
and promising future

"In this small book, Louay Safi has produced a mini-encyclopedia on the modern Holy Land, with profound historical and political analysis accompanied by handy maps, demographic charts, a glossary, and copies of all the relevant U.N. resolutions. This is ideal for both college students and knowledgeable policy advisers seeking to understand the challenges and opportunities in the Middle East today."

Robert Crane, Author and former Deputy Director (Planning),
U.S. National Security Council

"In this exposition, Louay Safi envisions a peaceful resolution of the Israeli-Palestinian Conflict rooted in a new political system that transcends liberal democracy and the ethnically exclusive nation state. Combining international laws and universally-sanctioned moral values, including sanctity of life, equal dignity, freedom of religion, democracy, and the rule of law, Safi's arguments capture the historic injustices and the Palestinian tragedy in the last century and masterfully illustrates how Zionist expansionist ideology has turned both Palestinians and Israeli Jews into victims of the belief that 'might makes right.' This monograph is among the few writings that succinctly narrate the century-long-conflict dynamics and identify the failing elements of the many political initiatives and agreements. The author's visionary call to abandon past and existing power frameworks and adopt prophetic principles of equality and human dignity is long past due for Palestinians, Israelis, and the global community as well."

Dr. Mohamed Abunimer, Professor of Peace and Conflict Studies
and Director of Salam Institute,
American University, Washington, DC

"The Israeli-Palestinian conflict is often falsely depicted as a religious conflict. In reality, it arose as a nationalist conflict in the context of late 19th and first half of the 20th century, in the broader matrix of colonial and post-colonial politics. While religion did not cause this conflict, it may well be a part of its solution. This monograph is a passionate yet level-headed call for justice that appeals to the best and noblest aspects of religious traditions to bring sanity, compassion, and peace to this crucial region."

Dr. Omid Safi, Professor of Religious Studies,
University of North Carolina

"The Israeli-Palestinian conflict is the longest running conflict in modern history, and is poisoning relations between the Arab and Muslim worlds and the West. Dr. Louay Safi makes some compelling arguments about how the one-state solution could work by giving Israelis and Palestinians equal rights under the law, and this idea needs to be carefully discussed and studied. Although major political and religious forces in both Israel and the Arab world are not likely to accept this solution, the main thesis of the book deserves serious consideration. It is time for Muslims, Christians, and Jews to work together for peace in the Holy Land to avoid further deaths and suffering on both sides."

Dr. Radwan Masmoudi, President of the Center for the
Study of Islam and Democracy

Preface

Palestine: Prophetic Principles over Prophecies outlines the emerging patterns of the struggle for freedom and justice; of unfulfilled promises, dashed hopes, untold misery, and the long search for the elusive peace in Palestine. For 60 years modern Israel flourished as the Palestinian pain and suffering grew, and Palestinian anger gave birth to new generations of fighters who draw meaning from their life of suffering by challenging the Israeli occupation.

As Israel, backed by western powers, pushes harder to assert its religious claims over Palestine, and as Palestinians, supported by Muslim societies, push back to assert their human and political rights, the Israeli-Palestinian Conflict becomes the epicenter of political pressure of great proportions that threatens to shake world peace to its foundation.

There is a great urgency to bring reason, justice, and humanity to the bloody and vicious exchange that dominates the Israeli-Palestinian Conflict. This monograph is an open call to end Palestinian suffering and prevent the impending earthquake from taking its ugly toll. It calls for rejecting parochial solutions inspired by historically-bound prophecies and faulty interpretations and for adopting solutions rooted in the prophetic principles of justice and compassion and in the universal commitment to human rights and dignity.

A lot of hope was pinned on the peace process that started in the early 1990's. The hope for just peace in which Palestinians would have a fair share of historical

Palestine has been replaced with dread and fear that the peace Israel is pursuing resembles the Roman Peace. The peace the Romans imposed throughout their Empire demanded a full submission from peoples who came under their domain. Ironically, it was the very peace that devastated early Jews and destroyed the last historical Jewish kingdom in Jerusalem. As the Roman poet Virgil described it, the Romans built their peace by "sparing the vanquished and crushing the proud."

It is this overreliance on force that is deeply troubling in the pursuit of Middle East Peace. It is always tempting for those who enjoy an overwhelming power to use it to solve conflicts. The power disparity between the Israelis and the Palestinians is very obvious, and Israel has not shied away from making this fact known to its Palestinian subjects.

Power is no panacea to solving conflicts particularly when human rights, dignity, identity, and honor are on the line. If history can teach us anything at all, it should teach us that the use of brutal power to privilege one community at the expense of the wellbeing of another undermines the power of the privileged and empowers the underprivileged. Israel itself after years of using power with impunity has started to feel the limits of power. To understand this fact of history is to understand the logic of history.

It is about time that a new vision is nurtured in the West about the future of the Middle East. Not only for the sake of the Palestinian community, but also for that of the Jewish community, a genuine and just peace must be pursued. It is about time that the Palestinian misery is put to an end and a new political dynamics is set in motion in the Middle East.

Table of Contents

Introduction

Sixty years have passed since Israel was founded in 1948 as a Jewish state in a predominantly Muslim region. The event represents a triumphant moment in the fulfillment of the Zionist dream to establish Palestine as a homeland for world Jewry. Zionism emerged in Europe in the age of rising nationalism and repeated anti-Semitic outbursts. The rise of Nazism in Europe and the persecution of European Jews by the Third Rich that dominated Europe from 1939 to 1945 pushed many European Jews to Palestine, which was then declared by the World Zionist Organization as "a country without people for a people without a country."

The establishment of a Jewish state in historical Palestine has been possible not only because of the ceaseless work of world Jewry, but also because of limitless support by Western powers. Western powers saw in the creation of Israel a desired solution for European anti-Semitism that culminated in the Jewish Holocaust. For sixty years, Israel has received crucial economic, political, and military support. Britain used its mandate over Palestine to facilitate the settlement of over 400,000 Jews between 1922 and 1946 (See Appendix 3). The United States alone has provided $156 billion in direct aid since 1947.

Sadly, the solution for European anti-Semitism and the efforts to end the Jewish suffering in Europe was achieved at the expense of the Palestinians. For Palestinians, as for Arabs and Muslims throughout the world, the founding of Israel has substituted the suffering of one people for another. Neighboring Arab countries rejected the partition of Palestine into Arab and Jewish states, and fought side by side with Palestinians to prevent the founding of Israel in 1948. They later fought five wars (1952, 1967, 1973, 1982, 2000, and 2006) to prevent its expansion and to force it to cede back territories it conquered in 1967 and 1982.

Although several Arab and Muslim governments have entered into peace treaties with Israel, and still others signaled their willingness to do the same, the official positions of these governments do not represent the sentiments and demands of their populations. Large majorities in countries that signed peace agreements with Israel, including Egypt and Jordan, are sympathetic to the plight of the Palestinians, and suspect of the intentions and dismiss of the moral claims of Israel.

The efforts to establish an exclusively Jewish state has been greatly troubling for Arabs and Muslims, particularly those who have wholeheartedly embraced the spirit of the age, which stresses the equal dignity of all people regardless of race, ethnicity, or religion. For the people of the Middle East, the insistence on giving American, European, or Russian Jews the "right of return" while denying it to those who were evicted from their homes or left them voluntarily to escape military conflict is a blatant exercise in double standards.

The discussion of the Israeli-Palestinian conflict raising a myriad of moral, legal, and historical issues, including the justification of an exclusively Jewish state, the transfer of Jews from various parts of the world to inhabit a country claimed by another people, the long-term viability of current arrangements, the impact of the current conflict on future relations between the East and the West, the religious duties and responsibilities of Muslims toward Palestine and the Palestinians, and the place of religious claims in the modern political order. I do not intend in this brief exposition to address all issues pertaining to the conflict. Rather, I will focus on delineating a principled approach to immediately address the crisis afflicting the lives of over five million Palestinians under Israeli occupation, and equal number in the Diaspora. I also stress the need to use one set of standards to treat Jews and Arabs as the only viable way to avoid turning the Israeli-Palestinian conflict into a global religious conflict.

The conflict in Palestine is gradually escalating into religious conflict among the followers of Judaism, Christianity, and Islam, thereby threatening world peace in ways that would undermine the long struggle to base politics on universal principles rather than religious affiliation. It has also emboldened religious fanatics in both the East and the West who seem eager to rebuild religiously exclusive political societies. This serious challenge requires all peoples to find ways to arrest a dangerous trend and reset human trajectory on a path that lead to the affirmation of the principles of equal rights and equal dignity of all persons and communities.

Palestine: Prophetic Principles over Prophecies highlights the moral underpinning of the Israeli-Palestinian Conflict. It does not provide specific solutions to the conflict but proposes the creation of a new political dynamics in the Middle East with the potential for bringing an amicable peace to the region. It calls on all people of conscience to work towards a political solution rooted in human rights and international humanitarian law. It stresses the need to recognize the equal dignity of all human beings, respect the universal principles at the core of modern consciousness, and forge a new political state suitable for the emerging global order.

This monograph calls, in short, for rejecting current political justification of the greatest injustice of our time based on parochial religious interpretations, and for adopting a solution rooted in the notions of equal dignity and universal rights. It calls, that is, for privileging prophetic traditions over prophecies!

1
In Search of Elusive Peace

"You, O Roman, remember to rule the nations with might.
This will be your genius--to impose the way of peace, to
spare the vanquished and crush the proud."
The Roman Poet Virgil

After four devastating wars that established its military dominance in the Middle East, Israel succeeded during the 1980s and 1990s in signing two major peace agreements with Egypt and Jordan, and began peace negotiations with the Palestinians. Jimmy Carter brokered the negotiation between Egypt and Israel that culminated in the Camp David Peace Accords. Bill Clinton led, during his presidency, two tracks of negotiations, one between Israel and the Palestinian Authority, and the other between Israel and Jordan. Jordan signed a peace agreement with Israel in 1994, but Palestinians and Israelis found no common ground. The Oslo Peace Negotiations began in earnest in 1993 and collapsed in 2000 just before President Clinton ended his second term in office.

George W. Bush, who succeeded Clinton, proposed in 2003 the boldest peace initiative of any American president to solve the Palestine issue, but managed to deliver only the most meager results during his two-term presidency. The Roadmap for Peace, developed by the United States in cooperation with Russia, the European Union, and the United Nations (the Quartet), was presented to Israel and the Palestinian Authority on April,

30 2003. Despite the proclaimed hopes, however, it has been a clear fiasco and anything but a roadmap to peace. Although the Bush administration, during its final year in power, organized the largest conference for Middle East peace ever assembled and again made the boldest promises, very few people are holding their breath. The Roadmap initiative is practically over, and all signs point to a dead-end.

Israel continues to confiscate more land and build more illegal settlements, while the Palestinians continue to hold onto their towns, villages, farmlands, and houses with all the strength they can muster. All participants in this widening confrontation keep digging themselves into a deeper hole and bringing the world to the brink of disaster. The disparity between the parties is great, outside help is increasingly favoring one party over the other, and no honest broker or visionary leader has yet appeared to take a principled stand and advance a fair solution.

At the heart of the deadlock in negotiating an agreeable peace between the Israelis and the Palestinians is a markedly different conception of peace. The Palestinians seek peace that brings complete control over the West Bank and Gaza based on the 1967 borders, prior to Israel's expansion beyond the territories it held then. They also insist on the right of return of all Palestinians to the towns and villages from which they were forced out in 1948. The Israelis, on the other hand, desire peace that transfers administrative control of Palestinian municipalities in the Occupied Territories to the Palestinian Authority. They also insist on controlling international borders, stationing large contingents of their forces in

Palestinian territories, and keeping the option of expanding settlements. (See Appendix 4 for further details)

How did the search for peace bring us to this sad state of affairs? Can the ongoing dynamic be changed from its current state to one that promotes real hope for peace? And what must be done to bring about a peaceful resolution to the Middle Eastern Conflict before it escalates into devastating wars whose impact can be felt far beyond the land of Palestine?

Two-State Solution and the Making of the Roadmap

I n his April 4, 2002 speech, President Bush outlined his formal position: a two-state solution that would result in an independent Palestinian state living "side by side" with a Jewish state in historical Palestine. "The Roadmap," he declared, "represents a starting point toward achieving the vision of two states, a secure State of Israel and a viable, peaceful, democratic Palestine. It is the framework for progress towards lasting peace and security in the Middle East. ..." A year later, the State Department produced a detailed plan with specific phases and benchmarks to guide the peace process and set 2005 as the year for achieving a "final and comprehensive settlement." The results are well known: illegal Israeli settlements continue to grow rapidly; the Palestinian Authority is divided into two; and Gaza is subject to repeated military assaults, starvation, and economic blockades by Israel.

The State Department's plan was in many ways an academic exercise, written with little attention to the dynamics of the political conflict that has gripped the region for the last sixty years.[1] The plan placed all the

---

[1]U.S. Department of State, Press Statement entitled "A Performance-Based Roadmap to a Permanent Two-State Solution to the Israeli-Palestinian Conflict," Washington, D.C., April 30, 2003

cards in the hands of the Israeli authorities, requiring the immediate and complete cessation of hostilities by Palestinians while permitting the Israeli military to continue its incursions into Palestinian towns and villages to arrest Palestinian activists and assassinate Palestinian militants. Mahmoud Abbas, excited by the Roadmap and what he believed to be a new commitment by the Bush administration to broker a new peace, persuaded Hamas to commit to a truce in May 2003. The truce lasted until August 21st, when, Israel, using an American made Apache, assassinated Ismail Abushanab. Abushanab was considered by many Palestinians to be a moderate who strongly supported the negotiated truce.[2]

Unlike his two predecessors, Jimmy Carter and Bill Clinton, who were deeply involved in negotiation, George Bush showed no interest in brokering a peace deal, leaving the matter completely in the hands of the Israeli government and the Palestinian Authority. Neither did any of the senior members of his administration get involved in sustained peace negotiations with the warring parties. The prospects for successful negotiations between the Israelis and the Palestinians received a serious setback when the Bush administration aligned itself completely with the Israeli negotiators who insisted that the Palestinian Authority dismantle resistance as a precondition for any Israeli concessions, even when the Israeli military refused to stop its frequent incursions into Palestinian territories.

---

[2] *Palestinian militants declare end to cease-fire*, CNN, August 21, 2003. Accessed on October 18, 2008.

The Bush administration saw no need to pressure the government of Ariel Sharon to stop Israeli incursions into Palestinian territories, and to at least freeze settlements as an important measure and first step to building trust. President Bush insisted that the United States cannot pressure the two parties to peace, and that future peace must evolve through negotiations and mutual agreements between the warring parties. This practically gave Israel the upper hand in deciding the future of the Roadmap, as it enjoyed overwhelming firepower.

The outcome of the Roadmap sponsored by the Bush administration is no different than the outcome of the Oslo Peace Process sponsored by the Clinton administration: more expansion and more resistance. The Israelis are determined to pursue the goal of a Greater Israel, and the Palestinians are increasingly willing to take strong punishments and heavy casualties to hold on to their land.

Moses' Mission and its Reenactment in Modern Times

The Jewish claim to Palestine is based on the divine promise to Abraham, a prophet claimed by the followers of Judaism, Christianity, and Islam: "On that day, God made a covenant with Abraham, saying: To your descendants I have given this land, from the river of Egypt as far as the great river the Euphrates. The land of the Kenites, Kenizzites, Kadmonite, the Chitties, Perizzites, Refraim, the Emorites, Canaanites, Girgashites and Yevusites." (Genesis 15:18-21)

The Promised Land was further specified during the time of Moses: "Now Moses went up from the plains of Moab to Mount Nebo, to the top of Pisgah, which is opposite Jericho. And the Lord showed him all the land, Gilead as far as Dan, and all Naphtali and the land of Ephraim and Manasseh, and all the land of Judah as far as the Western Sea, and the Negev and the plain in the valley of Jericho, the city of palm trees, as far as Zoar. Then the Lord said to him, this is the land which I swore to Abraham, Isaac, and Jacob, saying, 'I will give it to your descendants'; I have let you see with your eyes, but you shall not go over there." (Deuteronomy 34:1-4)

This second promise given in Deuteronomy evidently delineates a smaller expanse of land promised to Moses than the one promised to Abraham. The promise was fulfilled during the reign of Joshua, and reached its farthest expansion under Solomon when the Israelites controlled much of Greater Syria and parts of Iraq and southern Turkey.

Muslims do not disagree with the Biblical claims, as the Qur'an reaffirms God's promise to Moses that his followers will be delivered from their Egyptian servitude to the Holy Land.

"O my people! enter the holy land which God has assigned to you, and turn not back ignominiously, for then will you be overthrown, to your own ruin." They said: "O Moses! In this land are a people of exceeding strength: never shall we enter it until they leave it: if (once) they leave, then shall we enter." (Qur'an 5:21-22)

Their decision not to confront the tyrannical power that then controlled the Holy Land led to a forty-year wandering in the desert. Ultimately the Israelites entered the Holy Land under the leadership of Joshua and established a powerful Kingdom under Prophet David and Prophet Solomon. (Qur'an 2:249-251)

The Qur'an, however, treats the promise as a historical fact, particular to the Israelites, and not as a perpetual promise. When the Qur'an was revealed in the 7th century A.C., only a tiny Jewish population remained in the region where modern Palestine was demarcated by the British colonial power early in the 20th century. Palestine was predominantly Christian when Islam expanded throughout the region in the 7th century, four centuries after the Roman expulsion of the Jews.

While Muslims accept the divine promise to bequeath the Holy Land to the followers of Moses who were oppressed in Egypt, they do not accept the claim that a Biblical promise can be legitimately reenacted after thousands of years and used as a ground for gathering world Jewry in Palestine and dispossessing its current inhabitants of their ancestral land. Thus they consider such a deed to be a blatant violation of universally accepted moral principles and recognized international law. (see Appendix 1 & 2 for details)

The early pioneers of Zionist ideology, consumed with obtaining European Powers' endorsement of their demand for a Jewish homeland, hardly worried about Arab reaction. On August 29, 1897, they met in Basel, Switzerland, to refine their plan to take over Palestine. Imperial Europe, then expanding its colonial control into Asia and Africa, was forging new countries out of old ones and installing new regimes to replace fallen empires. In addition, the rise of European nationalism and the subsequent desire of European nations to affirm their national identity posed a serious challenge to European Jewry. Establishing a homeland in historic Palestine seemed to offer an effective solution to Europe's chronic anti-Semitism and fulfill a century-old Jewish longing for the Holy Land.

On November 2, 1917, the Zionist Organization extracted the Balfour Declaration, which recognized Palestine as a Jewish homeland. In 1919, it submitted a six-point proposal to the Peace Conference of Paris for establishing a Jewish Palestine. Two points were particularly notable: the boundaries of Palestine would "extend on the west to the Mediterranean, on the north to the Lebanon, on the east to the Hedjaz railway and the Gulf of Akabah," and the League of Nations was called upon to make Palestine a British mandate.

The prospect of a Jewish homeland brought great excitement to Zionist leaders, as they realized that their dream was being transformed into reality before their eyes. Many Zionist leaders did not fully grasp the direction of world history and the full consequences of reliving an ancient prophecy in modern times. Zionist leaders underestimated the reaction of the local population of Palestine, the Arab Middle East, and the rest of the Muslim world, to the formation of a Jewish State in the region. In an article by H. Sacher, published in the Atlantic Monthly in 1919 under the title "A Jewish Palestine," the author, a Jewish Historian, argued in support of the founding of a Jewish State, and envisaged a harmonious and peaceful society in which all live together well. Jewish Palestine, he insisted, "will do justice between all the nationalities within its borders. It will establish the equality of men and men, and work toward democracy, political and economic. It will be one of the pillars of the League of Nations, and by its relationship to all the scattered communities of Israel, it will forge powerful links for the brotherhood of the peoples. In the Near East and the Middle East it will strive to replace the broken tyranny of the Turk by a harmonious cooperation between Jew, Arab, and Armenian."[3]

Sacher saw in Palestine a place for self expression of religious and national identity long denied to European Jewry. Sacher portrayed the impact of an independent homeland on ordinary Jews in ways that revealed the impact of the homogenizing modern state and culture. "There he will see the Jewish faith developing freely," he pointed out, "according to the law of its being, distracted

---

[3] H. Sacher, "*A Jewish Palestine*," *The Atlantic Monthly*, July 1919

neither by opposition, nor by surrender to an alien environment. There he will see the Jewish national spirit expressing itself in a society modeled on the Jewish idea of justice, in a Hebrew literature, in a Hebrew art, in the myriad activities which make the life of a people on its own soil, under its own sky."

4
Reality Check and Emerging Demography

The sixty years that passed since the founding of the State of Israel have been traumatic, particularly for the Palestinian people, but increasingly to the world community. The migration of European Jews to Palestine began in earnest under the British mandate, and as the number of Jewish settlements in Palestine multiplied, Palestinians revolted repeatedly against Britain, in unsuccessful bids to gain independence. (See Appendix 3) Independence was instead handed to the Zionist organization, which in 1948 declared the birth of the State of Israel. The war of independence, which was fought mainly against Arab militias, led to the displacement of 711,000 Palestinians, mostly in surrounding Arab countries.

Today, more than 5 million Palestinians live in Diaspora mostly in Jordan, Syria, and Lebanon. Significant Palestinian communities also reside in the Gulf countries, Egypt, North Africa, and North America. These Palestinians are the subject of a debate over the "Palestinian right of return." Israel continues to resist demands to allow Palestinians who were forced out during this war, which Arabs call al-Nakba (the Catastrophe), to return on the grounds that doing so would disturb the existing "demographic balance" and make the claim of a Jewish state unsustainable. Indeed, this fear seems to be the main reason why Israel has been reluctant to formally annex the West Bank and Gaza. Such an act would also violate international law (See Appendix 1 & 2). But Israel has consistently violated U.N. Security Council resolutions when they clashed with its own designs, such as its formal annexation of Syria's Golan Heights even though the United Nations considers such an annexation to be illegal.

Despite the exhaustive negotiations for peace of the last two decades, Israel continues to push towards achieving the Zionist dream of Greater Israel. The Roadmap announced by Bush in January 2002 and his attempt to reinvigorate it in the last days of his administration during his visit to the Middle East in November 2008, are the continuation of countless rounds of negotiations during the nineties. Bill Clinton led a series of negotiations as part of the Oslo Agreement that aimed at establishing Palestinian state. The negotiations failed in 2000, when it became clear that the outcome was far removed from the claims of a sovereign state and contiguous territories. Camp David eventually gave the Palestinians a disarmed set of Bantustans under de facto Israeli control. (See Appendix 4)

Throughout the last two decades the Israelis negotiated with their Arab peace partners in bad faith. They continued to build more settlements, confiscate more land, and strengthen their grab over the territories as they engaged Palestinians in peace negotiations on the promise of Palestinian independence. Between 1993 and 2006, the number of settlers in the West Bank and Gaza doubled. The number of West Bank settlers increased from 116,000 in 1993 to 234,487 in 2004. 2006 statistics shows that the number of settlers has exceeded 268,400.

The number of settlers in Gaza jumped from 4,800 in 1993 to 7,826 in 2004, to drop to zero after the Israeli unilateral withdrawal from the Gaza strip in 2006.

Jewish settlements in the West Bank are illegal under International law. Article 49, paragraph 6 of the Fourth Geneva Convention states: "The Occupying Power shall not deport or transfer parts of its own civilian population into the territory it occupies". (See Appendix 2 for more details) The International Court of Justice has, likewise, asserted in paragraph 120 of its Advisory Opinion of July 9, 2004, that the settlements are illegal.

Jewish settlements also contradict the very spirit of Oslo and the Roadmap, which the United States considers to be the basis for ending the Israeli-Palestinian conflict. The Roadmap document published by the State Department in 2003 insists that "The settlement will resolve the Israeli-Palestinian conflict, and end the occupation that began in 1967, based on the foundations of the Madrid Conference, the principle of land for peace, UNSCRs 242, 338 and 1397, agreements previously reached by the parties, and the initiative of Saudi Crown Prince Abdullah – endorsed by the Beirut Arab League Summit in March 2002 – calling for acceptance of Israel as a neighbor living in peace and security, in the context of a comprehensive settlement."

5
Palestinian Misery and Double Standards

Sacher's vision of Israel that "will do justice between all the nationalities within its borders," has faded away. Palestinians who live in the West Bank and Gaza are deprived of their basic human rights, and are subjected to a set of standards that is far removed from the ones administered in the Israeli settlements. The Israeli government applies Israeli law to the settlers and the settlements, practically annexing them to the State of Israel. The Separation Wall serves as an instrument for such annexation. The resulting system is a regime of legalized separation and discrimination. This regime permits the co-existence of two independent legal systems in the same territory, with the rights of individuals determined on the basis of their religious affiliation. Palestinians who apply for building permits are often turned down, and when they build without building permits their houses are demolished by the Israeli Civil Administration, even when the construction is done on private land.

The Israeli Civil Administration facilitates, on the other hand, the construction of Jewish settlements and by-pass roads, even when these encircle Palestinian towns and villages, and make movement in the West Bank extremely difficult. In the last eight years, the numerous check points that were constructed in the West Bank (and Gaza until the Israeli Unilateral withdrawal) have made the life of Palestinians miserable, and destroyed the already weak Palestinian economy.

The squeeze policy adopted by the Israeli government against Palestinians did not stop at denying permits for new housing, but extends to confiscation of Palestinian land. The construction of what Israel calls the Security Barrier, and what its critics refer to as the Apartheid Wall, is being used to confiscate Palestinian lands, and has often resulted in separating families and occasionally making commuting between Palestinian localities impossible.

The Israeli government continued to confiscate land (more than 50,000 acres between 1993-1999), demolish Palestinian houses, and permit new settlements. At the height of its peace negotiation with the Palestinian National Authority in 1997, Israel doubled the number of construction permits it gave to Jewish settlers from 494 to 743 (a 50% increase). Evidence shows that under the dovish Barak the Israeli government escalated the building of Jewish settlements. The Associated Press reported on March 1, 1998, that "[a] confidential Housing Ministry report says there are more than 700 empty mobile homes in Jewish settlements in the West Bank, yet the government has allocated 300 more."[4]

Somaia Barghouti, Chargé d'affaires of the Permanent Observer Mission of Palestine to the United Nations, protested in a letter to the U.N. Secretary General, on January 26, 2005, against the continuous confiscation of Palestinian land for no avail. "Israeli bulldozers,"

---

[4] *Israeli Settlements on Palestinian Land* Report, published by *If America knew*, May 2002. Accessed October 26, 2008

Prophetic Principles over Prophecies

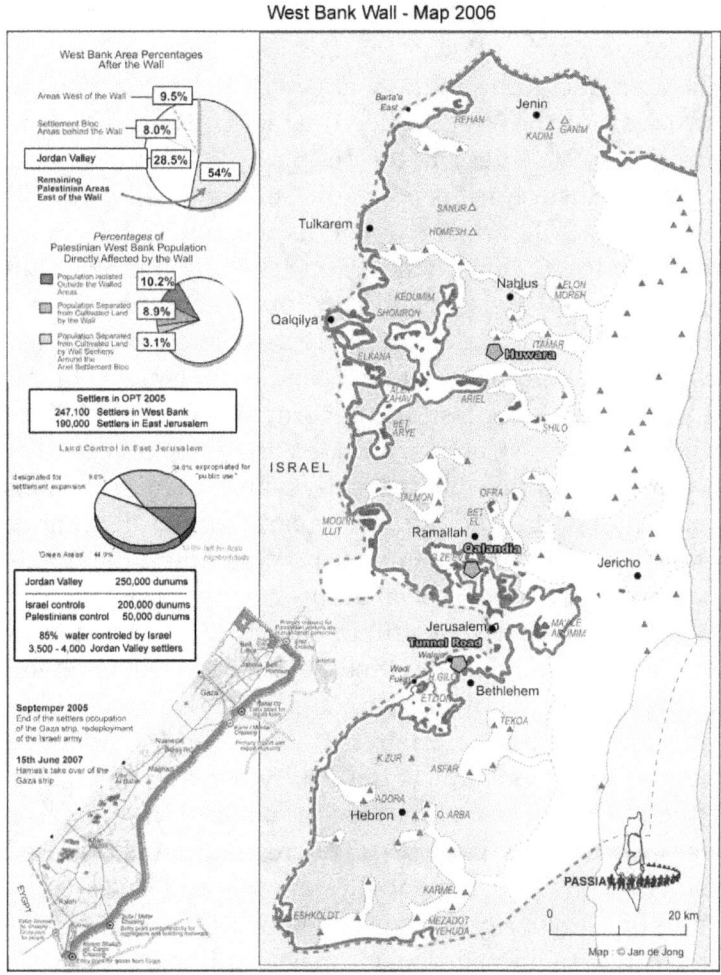

West Bank Wall - Map 2006

Map of the Wall that Israelis call "Defense Fence" and Palestinians describe as "Apartheid Wall"

Source: Palestinian Academic Society for the Study of International Affairs, Jerusalem / Al-Quds

Barghouti stressed, "have been razing land, confiscated by the occupying Power from its Palestinian owners, in the area, including in the village of Iskaka, for the construction of the Wall. Indeed, Israel continues to construct the Wall despite the ruling by the International Court of Justice, in its advisory opinion of July 9, 2004 (A/ES-10/273 and Corr.1), on its illegality." Barghouti went on to say "that Israel's construction of the Wall in the Occupied Palestinian Territory, including in and around East Jerusalem, and its associated regime are contrary to international law," and that "Israel is under an obligation to cease its construction of the Wall, to dismantle the structure situated therein, to repeal or render ineffective all legislative and regulatory acts relating thereto, and to make reparation for all damage caused by the construction of the Wall. Regrettably, the occupying Power has been doing exactly the opposite."[5]

Yet confiscation of land in violation of Geneva Convention goes unabated with little attention and condemnation by world powers and the United Nations. The last time Israel was criticized by an international body for its human rights violation was in 2000 when the UN Human Rights Commission adopted a resolution that condemned Israel's excesses. The resolution denounced Israel for the "widespread, systematic, and gross violations of human rights perpetrated by the Israeli occupying power, in particular mass killings, collective

---

[5] Excerpts from the letter that was submitted to the United Nations's Security Council and the General Assembly, published on the website of the United Nations Information System on the Question of Palestine (UNISQP), http://domino.un.org/unispal.nsf/, accessed on September 12, 2008. The full text of the letter is also provided in Appendix 5.

punishments, such as demolition of houses and closure of the Palestinian territories, measures which constitute war crimes and flagrant violation of international humanitarian law and crimes against humanity."

The resolution passed by a small margin. Nineteen states, mainly Arab and Islamic, as well as Cuba and China, voted in favor, while European and American states voted against it. Seventeen states abstained. The vote patterns reveal another irony of modern international politics: states who voted to uphold the human rights of the Palestinians are those who are often guilty of violating the human rights of their citizens, while the foremost advocates of international human rights stood in defense of the Israeli occupation.

Israel's ambassador Yaakov Levy denounced the resolution as "partisan, one sided, and inflammatory." This is because, he explained, there was "no call on the Palestinian side to stop the violence and rioting." Levy's indignation was echoed by the American and European envoys. Nancy Rubin, the U.S. envoy, rejected the resolution's language as "one-sided and vituperative." Rubin's argument is not that the state of Israel is innocent of the "war crimes" and the "crimes against humanity" attributed to it, but that the language is blunt and direct, and was hence disturbing. In a sense Rubin is right: the description of Israel's common practices against the Palestinians are at odd with its image in Western media. Yet neither Levy nor Rubin could deny that Israel is guilty of the practices attributed to it in the Human

Rights Commission's resolution, practices which international law classify as "crimes against humanity."

French envoy Philippe Petit who negotiated hard on behalf of the European Union to tone down the resolution's language explained the European bloc vote against it: "the commission's duty," he stressed, "was to defend human rights worldwide, not make 'political denunciation'." Put more precisely, the Commission should pay attention to violation of human rights everywhere in the world except in the state of Israel.

6
Logic of History and Power

Modern Israel's predicament is not easy to miss: a nation created to liberate European Jewry from discrimination and oppression is increasingly guilty of the very practices it sought to escape. This reality has brought anguish even to many Jews. For decades, Israeli leaders have tried to use the country's military advantage to force Arab and Palestinian compliance. This worked for a while, as the early Zionist pioneers faced vanquished and illiterate Arab communities. But the policies of iron fists and excessive force by successive Israeli regimes have backfired. Israel is increasingly facing new generations of Palestinians who are determined to reclaim their honor and dignity and who are willing to risk their lives and pay a high cost to achieve freedom and self-determination.

Some Israeli leaders have begun to realize that traditional approaches aimed at forcing the Palestinians to surrender to the Zionist project of Greater Israel no longer work. In a *New York Times* article of August 14, 2005, Ethan Bronner quoted a senior Israeli official closely associated with Likud leaders as saying: "The fact that hundreds of them are willing to blow themselves up is significant. We didn't give them any credit before. In spite of our being the strongest military power in the Middle East, we lost 1,200 people over the last four years.

It finally sank in to Sharon and the rest of the leadership that these people were not giving up."[6]

During December 2003, then Deputy Prime Minister Ehud Olmert told Nahum Barnea of *Yediot Aharonot*: "Israel will soon need to make a strategic recognition. ... We are nearing the point where more and more Palestinians will say: 'We're persuaded. We agree with [right-wing politician Avigdor] Lieberman. There isn't room for two states between the Jordan and the sea. All we want is the right to vote.' On the day they reach that point," said Olmert, "we lose everything. ... I quake to think that leading the fight against us will be liberal Jewish groups that led the fight against apartheid in South Africa."[7] Now serving as Israel's prime minister, he repeated his concerns, albeit in more ambiguous language, upon his return from the Annapolis Conference by telling *Haaretz* on November 28, 2007, that "the State of Israel cannot endure unless a Palestinian state comes into being."

Five years later, the two-state solution remains elusive. Pragmatic Israeli leaders have not been able to revise the logic of return. If modern Israel is a fulfillment of a divine promise, it is difficult to argue against Greater Israel. Many Palestinians, Arabs, and Muslims have developed profound doubts as to Israel's intentions and final borders. Many in the Middle East suspect that Israel

---

[6] Ethan Bronner , "Why 'Greater Israel' Never Came to Be?," New York Times" (14 Aug. 2005) article,
http://www.nytimes.com/2005/08/14/weekinreview/14bron.html?_r=3&pagewanted=print&oref=slogin&oref=slogin&oref=slogin
[7] Yacov Ben Efrat, "The Fading of the Two-State Solution," *The Challenge*, no. 107, Jan.-Feb 2008.

still wants to fulfill the Biblical boundaries of Greater Israel, which extend far beyond modern Palestine. The late Yaser Arafat and Hafiz al-Assad are on record as protesting Israel's design to expand its boundaries to Lebanon, Syria, and even Iraq. In a special meeting with the U.N. Security Council in Geneva in September 1988, Arafat produced a document that "proved" Israel's expansionist goals: "This document is a 'map of Greater Israel' which is inscribed on this Israeli coin, the 10-agora piece." Describing Israel's boundaries as they appeared on that map, Arafat stressed that they include "all of Palestine, all of Lebanon, all of Jordan, half of Syria, two-thirds of Iraq, one-third of Saudi Arabia as far as holy Medina, and half of Sinai." (Middle East Quarterly, March 1994).

Commenting on Arafat's argument, Daniel Pipes, the neoconservative American historian and analyst of the Middle East, rejected the contention that the Greater Israel espoused by modern Zionism encompasses Syria and Jordan. Conceding that modern Zionist leaders and historians, including Theodor Herzl, made references to Jewish settlements in Syria and Jordan, Pipes insisted that these were personal views and do not represent established views on Israel's borders. Along with many other conservative Jews, however, he insists that Gaza and the West Bank must be within Israel's borders.

While most Israelis are increasingly aware that using force has certain limitations and seem willing to compromise with Palestinians, a determined minority represented by the Likud and the ultra-religious parties is bent on pushing all the way. Avigdor Lieberman, leader of the Right-wing Yisrael Beiteinu party, resigned from

Olmert's cabinet during January 2008 to protest the renewal of peace talks with the Palestinian Authority that seek to address Jerusalem's final status. The Israeli Right's position has strong support in the United States. Conservative American Jewish and Christian organizations have consistently backed the Likud and advocated a Greater Israel that extends to the West Bank and Gaza.

In 1996, several leading American neoconservatives, among them Richard Perle (Pentagon policy adviser [resigned February 2004] and former Likud policy adviser), James Colbert (communications director, Jewish Institute for National Security Affairs), Charles Fairbanks, Jr. (former deputy assistant secretary in the U.S. Department of State), Douglas J. Feith (former undersecretary of defense for policy), and Robert Loewenberg (founder, Institute for Advanced Strategic & Political Studies [IASPS-Jerusalem]), authored "A Clean Break: A New Strategy for Securing the Realm," which was published by the Israeli-based IASPS. This political blueprint, meant for the incoming government of Benjamin Netanyahu, rejected the Oslo peace process and reasserted Israel's claim to the West Bank and Gaza. Furthermore, it called for rejecting the principle of trading land for peace, established by the Oslo Agreement, and demanded the unconditional Palestinian acceptance of Likud's terms (peace for peace), removing Saddam Hussain from power, and reconstituting Iraq.

The two-state solution has another aspect: the 5 million Palestinians living in the Diaspora, well-organized and strongly committed to their ancestral land, have organized their lives around the dream of return. In an essay entitled "It Is Always Eid in Palestine," Yasmine

Ali, a Palestinian-American who visited a Palestinian refugee camp in 1999, describes her encounter with elementary students who have never seen Palestine: "… what really caught my eye was the 'Wall Magazine,' which consisted of writings by Shatila children. There were several pages tacked to the bulletin board, listing qualities that the children had, in their minds, attributed to Palestine: 'Palestine is a very, very beautiful land … There is a sea of chocolate in Palestine … Children are always happy in Palestine … Women don't gossip in Palestine … The streets are very clean in Palestine … It is always Eid ["Feast Day"] in Palestine … Parents don't die in Palestine.' I stared at that for a long time. It was indescribably poignant, how this obviously reflected their situation in Shatila camp. It reminded me of how the Jews in the ghettos of Poland and Germany and numerous other countries used to imagine Palestine as the Promised Land -- indeed, how it has been imagined by so many the world over for thousands of years. And now by Palestinians themselves. Palestine, the Promised Land, once and forever. The irony was too bitter."[8]

---

[8] Remembering Shatila: "It Is Always Eid in Palestine," published online at http://www.adc.org/action/2000/16september2000.htm. Accessed on October 3, 2008.

7

From Power Play to Common Principles

"[The Zionists pioneers believed that] the only language the Arabs understand is that of force," wrote Ahad Ha'Am, the leading Eastern European Jewish essayist, upon returning from a visit to Palestine in 1891. Throughout all of its conflicts with neighboring Arab countries, Israel has always had the advantage of superior fighting force. For decades it has succeeded in advancing its claims to Palestine by creating facts on the ground. In addition to a superior military that has acquired a reputation of invincibility, the construction zeal of Jewish settlements in the Holy Land has allowed Israel to grow and expand. For decades, fighting and building was done with great religious zeal.

Years of Israeli mastery over Palestinians and the constant reliance on force to keep them in check have led to similar perceptions among Palestinians: that force is the only option available to counter Israeli expansion. The Israeli occupation has transformed the Palestinians, bringing about a generation of angry and determined militants convinced that the only language Israel understands is that of force.

Force, however, does not bring a permanent and long lasting solution to conflicts. "Might does not make right," is a principle borne by long, and regrettably repeated, historical experience. "The strongest is never strong enough to be always the master," observed Rousseau in his Social Contract, "unless he transforms strength into right, and obedience into duty."[9] Israel has been expanding its domain not on the basis on any established system of law, but by the overwhelming power it has over ordinary Palestinians and its ability to create facts on the ground. The biblical account and historical grievances stem from the experience of the European Jewry, which is the basis of Western support, has not been accepted by Middle Eastern societies. The people of the Middle East see the divine promise as historically bound, and expect to be treated as people with equal rights and dignity.

The impetus that drives the Israeli-Palestinian Conflict is rooted in the international struggle of the 18th and 19th centuries Europe, and has nothing to do with the logic of international relations based on the notion of right and international law expected by the citizens of the 21st century. The logic that guided the establishment and expansion of Israel has focused more on the affirmation of Jewish identity and power, and less on justice and the right of Palestinians. This logic can be seen in the arguments of the foremost Zionist leader of the 20th Century. "[T]hese days it is not right but might which prevails," noted David Ben-Gurion. "It is more important to have force than justice on one's side," he added. He went on to say that in a period of "power politics, the powers that become hard of hearing respond only to the roar of

---

[9] Jean-Jacques Rousseau, The Social Contract (London, UK: Maurice Cranston, 1968)

cannons. And the Jews in the Diaspora have no cannons."[10]

Europe has already turned the page on its nationalist politics and colonial ambitions, while the Middle East is still engulfed in destructive wars rooted in religious differences and national aspirations. Furthermore, the appeal to religion for establishing political structures has inspired other actors to privilege religious affiliation over a system of rights and law. The Israeli-Palestinian conflict, if not quickly resolved, threatens to galvanize the world along religious lines and transform itself into a global conflict.

Muslim militants throughout the world have already used Palestine as a central issue to galvanize support, and far Right groups in the West use the same issue to mobilize the West against Islam and Muslims. There is a dire need to begin a rational debate on how to address the Palestinian question calmly and on the basis the political values of justice, equality, democracy, and freedom.

---

[10] Shabtai Teveth, *Ben Gurion and the Palestinian Arab* (Oxford University, 1985)

8
Globalizing the Conflict

Not only did Israel fail to "establish the equality of men and men," as Sacher had hoped it would when he published his vision of a Jewish Palestine nearly a century ago, it also failed to "replace the broken tyranny of the Turk by a harmonious cooperation between Jew, Arab, and Armenian." Sacher the historian failed to anticipate the extent of the Arabs' and Muslims' resistance to the creation of an exclusively Jewish state. The reality is that since its inception, Israel has been engaged in numerous hostile exchanges with its neighbors. While it has managed to neutralize some old enemies, most notably the PLO, Egypt, and Jordan, it has created new and even fiercer ones, including Hamas, Hizballah, and Iran. Its peace with Egypt and Jordan remains quite fragile, resting as it does on the ability of two undemocratic regimes to keep their populations silent – populations whose popular sentiments have always been pro-Palestinian.

Israeli leadership has been forced to view any country in the region that expresses sympathy and support for the Palestinians as a potential enemy. Israel is constantly working to make sure that it is able to maintain a comfortable margin of military advantage. As a result, Israel has also felt duty-bound to check the rise of any military power in the region in order to ensure that its military superiority is never challenged. This has led to preemptive wars and strikes in the past against Egypt, Jordan,

Syria, Lebanon, and Iraq. Israel currently is urging the United States to undertake a preemptive military attack against Iran if it does not stop enriching uranium for fear that it can be used for military purposes, and has threatened that it will carry out the attack if need be.

In recent years, the Palestinian conflict has deepened the divide between predominantly Muslim and Western countries. A 2007 survey by Gallup showed that 58% of Americans are sympathetic to Israelis with only 20% expressing sympathy toward Palestinians. 44% thought that the United State should not get involved in any diplomatic efforts to end the conflict, unless Palestinians recognize Israel first, while 25% thought the United States should not do anything about it. 57% thought that the United States should not give any support to the Palestinian Authority, while 30% thought support must be contingent on recognizing Israel. This is quite different from the position found in Arab and Muslim countries, which have made repeated demands for immediate withdrawal of Israel from the territories it has occupied since 1967, and have frequently expressed resentment of American support for Israeli policies and measures against Palestinians.

For five years, nightly news programs in the Middle East have been bombarding their audiences with graphic pictures of the life in the West Bank and Gaza. Raids by the Israeli military on towns and villages, home demolitions, confiscation of land, assassination of militants, closures and blockades, impoverished and crowded neighborhoods, and similar images fill the TV screens on a daily basis. This has created deep bitterness and guilt as old and young helplessly watch Palestinian suffering.

The picture of the Middle East conflict is almost diametrically opposite across the West-Middle East divide.

9
Silencing Voices of Moderation

T here is little debate on the reality and consequences of the Israeli-Palestinian conflict. Jimmy
Carter pointed out in his recent book, *Palestine:
Peace Not Apartheid*, that the political debate about the
policies of the Israeli government is much more open and
lively in Israel than it is in the United States. "There are
constant and vehement political and media debates in
Israel concerning its policies in the West Bank," Carter
claimed, "but because of powerful political, economic,
and religious forces in the U.S., Israeli government
decisions are rarely questioned or condemned, voices
from Jerusalem dominate our media, and most American
citizens are unaware of circumstances in the occupied
territories."[11]

Several American political leaders and scholars blame
the lack of political debate and balanced media coverage
of the Israeli-Palestinian conflict on the Jewish Lobby, a
loose coalition of pro-Israel organizations devoted to
promoting Israeli interests. Carter himself felt the brunt
of the Lobby upon the publication of his recent book on
Palestine. The book was deemed by conservative Jewish
groups to be anti-Semitic because it expresses sympathy
for the plight of the Palestinians, and brought attention to

---

[11] Jimmy Carter, *Palestine: Peace Not Apartheid* (Simon & Schuster: 2006)

the Israeli politics that aim at fragmenting the Occupied Territories and subjugating the Palestinian people.

Another courageous attempt to stimulate the debate about Israel's policies in the Occupied Land and their consequences for the United States was made by the two foremost political scientists in the United States, John Mearsheimer and Stephen Walt. Their recent book, *The Jewish Lobby*, an expansion of a paper they published under the same title, brings to the fore the strategies employed by pro-Israel lobbyists, and unveils the extent of their influence on U.S. foreign policy toward the Middle East. One consequence of the Jewish Lobby's strategy illustrated by Mearsheimer and Walt is the "strong prejudice against criticizing Israeli policy," leading to a current situation whereby "putting pressure on Israel is considered out of order."[12]

The Jewish Lobby provides examples of pressure tactics employed by conservative Jewish groups to frustrate efforts by prominent American Jews to balance inhumane Israeli policies toward the Palestinians and curb the Israeli excesses. The book documents, for example, the backlash against Edgar Bronfman Sr., the president of the World Jewish Congress, for writing a letter to President Bush in 2003 urging him to persuade Israel to curb construction of its controversial "security fence". His critics accused him of "perfidy" and argued that "it would be obscene at any time for the president of the World Jewish Congress to lobby the president of the

---

[12] John Mearsheimer and Stephen Walt, *The Jewish Lobby* (Farrar, Straus, and Giroux: 2007)

United States to resist policies being promoted by the government of Israel."

Likewise, Seymour Reich the president of the Israel Policy Forum, was denounced and accused of being "irresponsible," for advising Condoleezza Rice in November, 2005, to ask Israel to reopen a critical border crossing in the Gaza Strip. His critics insisted that, "There is absolutely no room in the Jewish mainstream for actively canvassing against the security-related policies . . . of Israel." The severity of the attacks forced Reich to announce that "the word 'pressure' is not in my vocabulary when it comes to Israel."

10
Prospects for Just Peace

The conflict in Palestine threatens to destabilize world politics and embolden fundamentalist demands for religiously exclusive political states. The principle of the rule of law has suffered immensely under the climate of fear that followed the terrorist attacks on the American homeland on September 11, 2001. Extremists in both the East and the West are working hard to deepen the divide, and turn the Middle East conflict into an all-out religious war. The Israeli-Palestinian Conflict is being used by the far right in both Muslim and Western countries to justify bigotry and demonize people on the other side of the divide.

There is a dire need to use our creative energy to find a just and equitable solution to the conflict. The logic of "creating facts on the ground" and "might makes right" must give way to the spirit of the age, of equal dignity and the rule of law. It might well be the case that the conflict might continue to play itself out until complete victory or complete defeat is achieved. But this would definitely be a tragic moment, as it would signal the triumph of force over morality and rationality. It would be a tragic moment, because by then, the conflict would have created overwhelming misery on all sides that no human being would be willing to contemplate.

The solution to the conflict must not be based on Jewish, Christian, or Muslim prophecies that would only inflame hate and mistrust among the followers of the three religious traditions (See Appendix 6). It should, rather, be based on the prophetic principles cherished by the three religious traditions. It must be based on the shared committed to the sanctity of human life, and the universally accepted principles of equal dignity, freedom of religion, democracy, and the rule of law.

Ironically, applying the above criteria would inevitably lead us to the often dreaded one-state solution. Author Daniel Lazare, Israeli journalist Daniel Gavron, Palestinian negotiator Ahmad Khalidi, Tel Aviv University research director Gary Sussman, and Michael Tarazi, the legal advisor to the Palestinian Authority advocate a one-state solution. They have all argued that the two-state solution is not a viable option given the ever expanding Israeli settlements, the "security wall" Israel built on Palestinian land, and the web of Israeli-only highways that cut throughout the West Bank. These developments coupled with the rapid growth of the Arab-Israeli population shed serious doubt about the viability of the currently popular two-state solution among Western nations and several Arab nations.

There is, however, a serious reason why the one-state proposal may be more of an illusion than a solution within existing political paradigm. This proposed solution is not attractive to all the political movements locked in the Middle East Conflict: Arab nationalism, Islamism, and Jewish Nationalism. Arab nationalists and Islamists see Israel as an obstacle in the road to achieving Arab and Islamic unity. Jewish nationalism represented by Zionism sees, on the other hand, the one-state proposal as a serious setback to the Jewish aspiration to found a Jewish state where Jews can nurture their Jewish identity while allowing the religious members of the world Jewry to freely practice their religion.

Does this mean that there is no solution that can be found to satisfy the interests and aspirations of the warring parties in the Middle East? While I am aware that any solution must speak to a multiplicity of concerns, and it must not be based on purely abstract and theoretical considerations, I do believe that an amicable solution can be found and that the first step for doing that is to change the dynamics on the ground.

The new dynamics must be grounded in the universal principles widely accepted by all parties: equal dignity of all people regardless of their ethnic and religious backgrounds. These principles must be complemented by a long held tradition in the Middle East region that recognizes the moral and cultural autonomy of religious communities. The lack of religious and cultural autonomy under nineteenth-century European nationalism was a major force setting European Jews on a path to establish an exclusively Jewish state.

The current dynamics cannot be sustained for long because it is based on a logic that belongs to a different era in human evolution. It belongs to the age of prophets and prophecies. Prophetic logic requires prophets who can explain their actions and decision by reference to revelation and direct communication with God. All modern prophets are false prophets because they follow a logic they do not fully understand and cannot defend by reference to the principles of justice, equality, or established human rights that define legitimate political authority. Sustainable political claims in the 21st century must be rooted in universal principles that recognize the equal dignity of all peoples.

The first step to find an amicable solution to the Middle East conflict is to provide the Palestinians with equal political rights and equal access to state institutions while recognizing the rights of both Jews and Palestinians to have complete autonomy to set their own religiously and ethnically specific institutions and laws.

Creating new political dynamics would require a political system in which religious communities enjoy a much higher level of moral, legal, and political autonomy than is experienced in modern states, but this would be an experience worth taking as it might provide a new model for the emerging post-modern world order. Modern states are already strained and are increasingly becoming incapable of handling a new global order where diverse religious and ethnic traditions are sharing a diminishing global space.

Applying equality under the law at the state level would require that Palestinians who were forced from their land be permitted to return to their towns and villages. It would also mean the end of the Zionist dream of a purely Jewish State over all of historical Palestine. Many Jews in Israel and in Western societies are brought up believing in this dream. The idea of exclusive national states belongs to the nineteenth century, and the history of twentieth-century European wars illustrates that it is a self-destructive idea. The idea that a nation can respect the rule of law internally while treating the international arena as a "state of nature" has no place in a globalizing society where ethnic and religious exclusivity is vanishing quickly everywhere, and particularly in Western society.

This solution will not satisfy every political group in the Palestinian and Israeli population, and will be opposed fiercely by those who are driven by nationalist ambitions and by dreams about the elimination of their opponents. But those who harbor complete disdain for the other party represent fanatical fringe groups, while the majority in both camps may become inclined to pursue a solution rooted in their moral commitment and universally accepted values.

Mainstream Arabs and Jews are likely to choose a solution based on the principles of fairness, democracy, and human rights, and one that ensures equal dignity, due process, and political participation, over the call for complete victory or complete defeat at an extraordinary price of human suffering and death. A solution that protects religious freedom and identity while ensuring equal rights and dignity should be attractive to both Arabs and Jews for the following reasons:

1. It allows the Jews to live under conditions that promote both their Jewish identity and practices, and give Palestinians the opportunity to live a life of freedom and dignity away from the oppressive force of occupation.
2. The right of people to experience their collective identity freely under their own laws and religious teaching is unthinkable within the liberal democratic tradition, but quite acceptable for Muslim societies that have recognized the legal and moral autonomy of religious groups for a millennium.

3. The new arrangements will alter the dynamics of master and slave populations that have created deep hatred, disdain, and mistrust, and provide both Arabs and Jews with the opportunity to experience one another as human beings.
4. It will disarm the forces of polarization in Muslim and Western societies who seem to be happy to take advantage of the conflict as a means to undo the accomplishments of the last century that have allowed the advent of political societies governed by law and ruled by accountable governments.

Will the principles of fairness and equal dignity triumph over self-styled and self-fulfilled prophecies? We must admit that the odds against changing the political dynamics in the Middle East Conflict are great. Fear and anger tend to overwhelm hope, and winning wars is more glorious than making peace. Of Equal concern is the ability of the far right to use prophecies as justification for violating the principles of justice and compassion emphasized by the Prophets.

Our faith in the goodness of human nature and the power of transcendental principles and values should give us hope that the future is always on the side of those who stand for fairness and justice. The answer to the question hinges, however, on the actions of people of good will and deep faith across the religious and cultural divides.

We should both hope and pray that people of reason and deep faith will privilege the clear principles demanded by their religions and international conventions over vague prophecies interpreted by fallible, rationally limited, and emotionally charged human beings.

Appendix 1:

The United Nations Resolutions Concerning Palestine

Israel expansionist policies in Palestine are in violation of International Law and a long series of United Nations Resolutions. Below are a list of key UN Security Council resolutions demanding Israel withdrawal from the West Bank and Gaza, and establishing the right of return for Palestinians.

U.N. Resolution 181 II B – November 29, 1947
U.N. Resolution 242 - November 22, 1967
U.N. Resolution 338 - October 22, 1973
U.N. Resolution 465 - March 1, 1980
U.N. Resolution 681 – December 20, 1990

U.N. Resolution 181 II B

The north-eastern sector of the Jewish State (Eastern Galilee) is bounded on the north and west by the Lebanese frontier and on the east by the frontiers of Syria and Trans-jordan. It includes the whole of the Huleh Basin, Lake Tiberias, the whole of the Beisan Sub-District, the boundary line being extended to the crest of the Gilboa mountains and the Wadi Malih. From there the Jewish State extends north-west, following the boundary described in respect of the Arab State. The Jewish section of the coastal plain extends from a point between Minat El-Qila and Nabi Yunis in the Gaza Sub-District and includes the towns of Haifa and Tel-Aviv, leaving Jaffa as an enclave of the Arab State. The eastern frontier of the Jewish State follows the boundary described in respect of the Arab State.

The Beersheba area comprises the whole of the Beersheba Sub-District, including the Negeb and the eastern part of the Gaza Sub-District, but excluding the town of Beersheba and those areas described in respect of the Arab State. It includes also a strip of land along the Dead Sea stretching from the Beersheba-Hebron Sub-District boundary line to 'Ein Geddi, as described in respect of the Arab State.

U.N. Resolution 242

The Security Council, Expressing its continuing concern with the grave situation in the Middle East.

Emphasizing the inadmissibility of the acquisition of territory by war and the need to work for a just and lasting peace in which every state in the area can live in security.

Emphasizing further that all member states in their acceptance of the Charter of the United Nations have undertaken a commitment to act in accordance with Article 2 of the Charter

A. Affirms that the fulfillment of Charter principles requires the establishment of a just and lasting peace in the Middle East which should include the application of both the following principles:

1. Withdrawal of Israeli armed forces from territories of recent conflict.

2. Termination of all claims or states of belligerency and respect for and acknowledgement of the sovereignty, territorial integrity, and political independence of every state in the area and their right to live in peace within secure and recognized boundaries free from threats or acts of force.

B. Affirms further the necessity for:

1. Guaranteeing freedom of navigation through international waterways in the area.

2. Achieving a just settlement of the refugee problem.

3. Guaranteeing the territorial inviolability and political independence of every state in the area through measures including the establishment of demilitarized zones.

C. Requests the Secretary General to designate a special representative to proceed to the Middle East to establish and maintain contacts within the state concerned in order to promote agreement and assist efforts to achieve a peaceful and accepted settlement in accordance with the provisions and principles in this resolution.

U.N. Resolution 338

The Security Council,

1. Calls upon all parties to the present fighting to cease all fighting and to terminate all military activity immediately, no later than 12 hours after the movement of the adoption of this decision, in the positions they now occupy.

2. Calls upon the parties concerned to start immediately after the cease fire the implementation of Security Council resolution 242 (1967) in all of its parts.

3. Decides that, immediately and concurrently with the cease fire, negotiations shall start between the parties concerned to establish a just and a durable peace in the Middle East.

U.N. Resolution 465

The Security Council,

1. Affirming once more that the fourth Geneva Convention relative to the protection of civilian persons in time of war of 12 August 1949 is applicable to the Arab territories occupied by Israel since 1967, including Jerusalem.

2. Determines that all measures taken by Israel to change the physical character, demographic composition, institutional structure of status of the Palestinian and other Arab territories occupied since 1967, including Jerusalem, or any part thereof, have no legal validity and

that Israel's policy and practices of setting parts of its population and new Immigrants in those territories constitute a flagrant violation of the fourth Geneva convention relative to the protection of civilian persons in time of war and also constitute a serious obstruction to achieving a comprehensive, just and lasting peace in the Middle East.

3. Strongly deplores the continuation and persistence of Israel in pursuing those policies and practices and calls upon the government and people of Israel to rescind those measures, to dismantle the existing settlements and in particular to cease, on an urgent basis, the establishment, construction and planning of settlements in the Arab territories occupied since 1967, including Jerusalem.

4. Calls upon all states not to provide Israel with any assistance to be used specifically in connection with settlements in the Occupied Territories.

5. Requests the commission to continue to examine the situation relating to the settlements in the Arab territories occupied since 1967, including Jerusalem, to investigate the reported serious depletion of natural resources, particularly the water resources, with a view to ensuring the protection of those important natural resources of the territories under occupation, and keep under close scrutiny the implementation of the present resolution.

U.N. Resolution 681

The Security Council,

1. Expresses its grave concern over the rejection by Israel of Security Council resolutions 672 and 673.

2. Deplores the decision of the government of Israel to resume deportations of Palestinian civilians in the occupied territories.

3. Urges the government of Israel to accept de jure applicability of the Fourth Geneva Convention of 1949, to all the territories occupied by Israel since 1967, and to abide scrupulously by the provisions of the said convention.

4. Calls on the high contracting parties to the Geneva Convention to ensure respect by Israel for its obligations under the convention.

5. Requests the Secretary General, in co-operation with the International Committee of the Red Cross to develop further the idea from his report of convening a meeting of the high contracting parties, to discuss possible measures that might be taken by them under the convention.

6. Requests the Secretary General to monitor and observe the situation regarding Palestinian civilians under Israeli occupation, making new efforts in this regard on an urgent basis, and to utilize and designate or draw upon the United Nations and other personnel and resources present there in the area and elsewhere to accomplish this task, and to keep the Security Council regularly informed.

7. Requests further the Secretary General to submit a first progress report to the Security Council by the first week of March, 1991, and every four months thereafter.'

President's statement:
The members of the Security Council reaffirm their determination to support an active negotiating process in which all relevant parties would participate leading to a comprehensive, just and lasting peace to the Arab-Israeli conflict. In this context they agree that an international conference should facilitate efforts to achieve a negotiated settlement.

However, the members of the council are of the view that there is not unanimity as to when would be the appropriate time for such a conference.

In the view of the members of the council, the Arab-Israeli conflict is important and unique and must be addressed independently on its own merits.

Appendix 2

Geneva Convention on the Protection of Civilian Persons in Time of War

Selected Articles

The Geneva Convention was adopted on August 12, 1949 by the Diplomatic Conference for the Establishment of International Conventions for the Protection of Victims of War. It was held in Geneva from April 21 to August 12, 1949, and was put into force on October 21, 1950.

The Convention comprises 159 articles. The following articles represent those that are particularly relevant to the life of Palestinians under Israeli occupation. Article 2 stresses that all states are subject to the terms of the Convention, event those that are not signatories. Article 3 spells out the obligation of occupation forces to protect the life and dignity of the civilians under its occupation, regardless of ethnic and religious differences. Article 33 protects civilians under occupation against collective punishment, which the Israeli government regularly violates by demolishing the homes of the parents of presons implicated in attacks against Israel.

Finally, Article 49 outlaws the transfer of any population from their homes and guarantees the right of return of people who were forced to leave to their homes as a result of the conflict. Similarly, it outlaws any transfer of civilians of the occupying force to the occupied territories. Israel continues to violate this article by refusing to allow Palestinians who fled their towns and villages in 1948 to return, and by building settlements in occupied Palestine that are blatantly illegal under Geneva Convention.

Article 2
In addition to the provisions which shall be implemented in peacetime, the present Convention shall apply to all cases of declared war or of any other armed conflict which may arise between two or more of the High Contracting Parties, even if the state of war is not recognized by one of them.

The Convention shall also apply to all cases of partial or total occupation of the territory of a High Contracting Party, even if the said occupation meets with no armed resistance.

Although one of the Powers in conflict may not be a party to the present Convention, the Powers who are parties thereto shall remain bound by it in their mutual relations. They shall furthermore be bound by the Convention in relation to the said Power, if the latter accepts and applies the provisions thereof.

Article 3
In the case of armed conflict not of an international character occurring in the territory of one of the High Contracting Parties, each Party to the conflict shall be bound to apply, as a minimum, the following provisions:

1. Persons taking no active part in the hostilities, including members of armed forces who have laid down their arms and those placed hors de combat by sickness, wounds, detention, or any other cause, shall in all circumstances be treated humanely, without any adverse

distinction founded on race, color, religion or faith, sex, birth or wealth, or any other similar criteria.

To this end, the following acts are and shall remain prohibited at any time and in any place whatsoever with respect to the above-mentioned persons:

a. Violence to life and person, in particular murder of all kinds, mutilation, cruel treatment and torture;

b. Taking of hostages;

c. Outrages upon personal dignity, in particular humiliating and degrading treatment;

d. The passing of sentences and the carrying out of executions without previous judgment pronounced by a regularly constituted court, affording all the judicial guarantees which are recognized as indispensable by civilized peoples.

2. The wounded and sick shall be collected and cared for.

An impartial humanitarian body, such as the International Committee of the Red Cross, may offer its services to the Parties to the conflict.

The Parties to the conflict should further endeavour to bring into force, by means of special agreements, all or part of the other provisions of the present Convention.

The application of the preceding provisions shall not affect the legal status of the Parties to the conflict.

Article 33
No protected person may be punished for an offence he or she has not personally committed. Collective penalties and likewise all measures of intimidation or of terrorism are prohibited.

Pillage is prohibited.

Reprisals against protected persons and their property are prohibited.

Article 49

Individual or mass forcible transfers, as well as deportations of protected persons from occupied territory to the territory of the Occupying Power or to that of any other country, occupied or not, are prohibited, regardless of their motive.

Nevertheless, the Occupying Power may undertake total or partial evacuation of a given area if the security of the population or imperative military reasons do demand. Such evacuations may not involve the displacement of protected persons outside the bounds of the occupied territory except when for material reasons it is impossible to avoid such displacement. Persons thus evacuated shall be transferred back to their homes as soon as hostilities in the area in question have ceased.

The Occupying Power undertaking such transfers or evacuations shall ensure, to the greatest practicable extent, that proper accommodation is provided to receive the protected persons, that the removals are effected in satisfactory conditions of hygiene, health, safety and nutrition, and that members of the same family are not separated.

The Protecting Power shall be informed of any transfers and evacuations as soon as they have taken place.

The Occupying Power shall not detain protected persons in an area particularly exposed to the dangers of war unless the security of the population or imperative military reasons so demand.

The Occupying Power shall not deport or transfer parts of its own civilian population into the territory it occupies.

Appendix 3:
Demographic Change

The number of Jews who immigrated to Palestine during the British Mandate is astounding. The operation facilitated by Britain was so huge that it allowed more than 400,000 Jews to build new life in Palestine in the span of 26 years. The table below summarizes the transformation of Palestine into a Jewish State.

Population of Palestine, 1922-1942[a,b]

Year	Total	Muslims (No.)	(%)	Jews (No.)	(%)	Christians (No.)	(%)	Others (No.)	(%)
1922	752,048	589,177	78.34	83,790	11.14	71,464	9.50	7,617	1.01
1931	1,033,314	759,700	73.52	174,606	16.90	88,907	8.60	10,101	0.98
1931[c]	1,036,339	761,922	73.52	175,138	16.90	89,134	8 60	10,145	0.98
1932	1,073,827	778,803	72.52	192,137	17.90	92,520	8.61	10,367	0.97
1933	1,140,941	798,506	69.99	234,967	20.59	96,791	8.48	10,677	0.94
1934	1,210,554	814,379	67.27	282,975	23.38	102,407	8.46	10,793	0.89
1935	1,308,112	836,688	63.96	355,157	27.15	105,236	8.04	11,031	0.85
1936	1,366,692	862,730	63.13	384,078	28.10	108,506	7.94	11,378	0.83
1937	1,401,794	883,446	63.02	395,836	28.24	110,869	7.91	11,643	0.83
1938	1,435,285	900,250	62.72	411,222	28.65	111,974	7.80	11,839	0.83
1939	1,501,698	927,133	61.74	445,457	29.66	116,958	7.79	12,150	0.81
1940	1,544,530	947,846	61.37	463,535	30.01	120,587	7.81	12,562	0.81
1941	1,585,500	973,104	61.38	474,102	29.90	125,413	7.91	12,881	0.81
1942	1,620,005	995,292	61.44	484,408	29.90	127,184	7.85	13,121	0.81

a. Exclusive of members of His Majesty's Forces (Great Britain).

b. Adapted from table, "Estimated Population of Palestine," Statistical Abstract of Palestine 1943, p. 2.

c. The figures for 1931 and following years are as of December 31 of each year.

Source: Esco Foundation (1947).
(http://www.unu.edu/unupress/unupbooks/80859 e/80859E05.htm)

Appendix 4:

Israel Peace Offer of 2000

The Peace Process between Israel and the Palestinian Authority that followed the Oslo Agreement of 1993 culminated in a peace offer Israel made to the Palestinian Authority (PA) in 2000. The offer was rejected by the PA President Yasser Arafat. Bill Clinton blamed him for the failure of the peace negotiations.

The details of what was offered to the Palestinians emerged later and were summarized in the following map prepared by the Palestinian Academy Society for the Study of International affairs.

The text of the offer was never released to the public, leading to exchange of blames by the parties. The Israelis placed the blame on Arafat, and Bill Clinton who brokered the negotiations made a similar assessment as the following statement suggest: "I regret that in 2000 Arafat missed the opportunity to bring that nation into being and pray for the day when the dreams of the Palestinian people for a state and a better life will be realized in a just and lasting peace."

Arafat, on the other hand, insisted that he was offered cantons, small, isolated Palestinian islands, completely divided up by Israeli roads and settlements and surrounded by the Israelis. Details that were provided in later studies, including a book by Clayton Swisher published in 2004 under the title *The Truth About Camp David*, indicate that the offer fell far short from establishing an independent and viable state.

Projection of the West Bank Final Status Map presented
by Israel, Camp David, July 2000

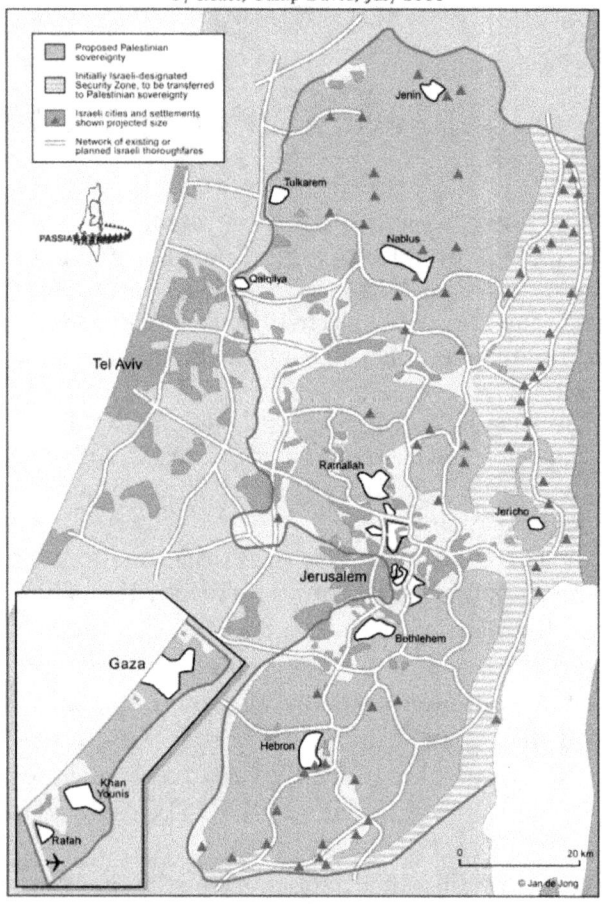

**Palestinian Academic Society for the Study of International Affairs
(PASSIA)**

Source: Palestinian Academic Society for the Study of International Affairs
(PASSIA), Jerusalem / Al-Quds.

Between 1946 and 2000 the Palestinians lost most of the land they once called their own. The following map tells the story.

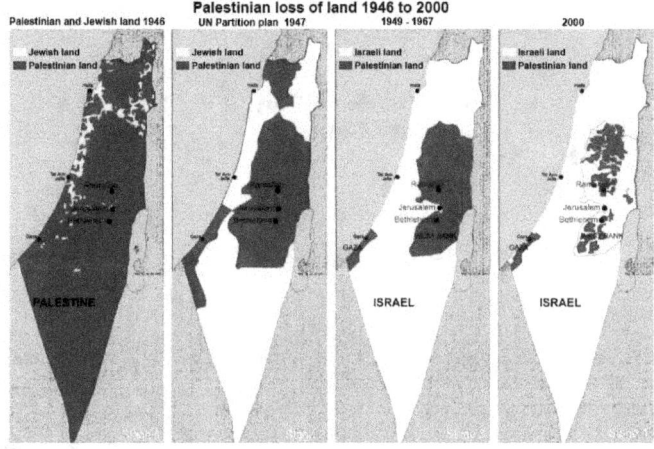

Palestinian loss of land 1946 to 2000

APPENDIX 5

UN REPRESENTATIVE OBSERVATIONS

 **General Assembly
Security Council**

Distr.
GENERAL

A/ES-10/290
S/2004/856
25 October 2004

Original: English

General Assembly
Tenth emergency special session
Agenda item 5
Illegal Israeli actions in Occupied
East Jerusalem and the rest of the
Occupied Palestinian Territory

Security Council
Fifty-ninth year

**Identical letters dated 25 October 2004 from the
Chargé d'affaires a.i. of the Permanent Observer
Mission of Palestine to the United Nations addressed
to the Secretary-General and the President of the
Security Council**

Israel, the occupying Power, continues its rampage of
carnage and destruction in the Occupied Palestinian
Territory. In the one week that has passed since our
last letter to you, the Israeli occupying forces have
brutally killed another 31 Palestinians, including

children, and seriously wounded dozens of other people. The occupying Power has persisted in particular with its military raids and attacks on civilian areas in the Gaza Strip, causing even more devastation in this already impoverished and desperate area.

Today, the Israeli occupying forces launched a large-scale military attack on the Khan Younis refugee camp in Gaza, terrorizing the civilian population and causing more death and destruction. Israeli tanks and armored vehicles raided the camp during the night and attacked the area from both the air and ground with missile strikes, tank shelling and gunfire. This excessive, indiscriminate and deliberate use of force by the occupying Power resulted in the killing of 16 Palestinians, including two children, today alone and the injury of more than 70 Palestinians, many of them critically wounded. Israeli bulldozers also demolished a home in the camp, crushed a wall around a hospital and caused damage to several other homes and properties.

The occupying Power has also continued its criminal practice of extrajudicial killing. On Thursday, 21 October, the Israeli occupying forces targeted and killed Yehia Adnan Mahmoud Jaber Al-Ghoul in a helicopter missile strike on his car outside a mosque in Gaza City just after evening prayers. One other man was killed in the strike and several other people were wounded.

As the annexed list of martyrs tragically illustrates, every single day Palestinian families are mourning the loss of their loved ones at the hands of a ruthless and brutal occupying Power. Indeed, not a day goes by in which Israel, the occupying Power, does not commit widespread and grave violations of the rights of the Palestinian people in the Occupied Palestinian Territory, including East Jerusalem. War crimes are being committed, State terrorism is being committed and systematic human rights violations are being committed by the occupying Power as it continues to breach all of its obligations under international law, including in particular under the Fourth Geneva Convention. The Palestinian people continue to look towards the international community to help bring an end to this horrific situation to which they are being subjected under Israeli occupation. The continuation of the current situation can only lead to more strife, bloodshed and loss for the Palestinian people and to greater instability in the area and in the region as a whole.

The present letter is in follow-up to our previous 208 letters to you regarding the ongoing crisis in the Occupied Palestinian Territory, including East Jerusalem, since 28 September 2000. These letters, dated from 29 September 2000 (A/55/432-S/2000/921) to 18 October 2004 (A/ES-10/289-S/2004/824) constitute a basic record of the crimes committed by Israel, the occupying Power, against the Palestinian people since September 2000. For all of these war crimes, State terrorism and systematic human rights violations committed against the Palestinian people, Israel, the occupying Power, must be held accountable and the perpetrators must be brought to justice.

Accordingly, in follow-up to the above-mentioned letters, it is my regret to inform you that, since my last letter to you, at least 31 more Palestinians have been killed by the Israeli occupying forces, raising the total number of martyrs killed since September 2000 to 3,439. (The names of the martyrs that have been identified are listed in the annex to the present letter.)

I would be grateful if you would arrange to have the text of the present letter and its annex distributed as a document of the tenth emergency special session of the General Assembly, under agenda item 5, and of the Security Council.

(Signed) Somaia **Barghouti**
Chargé d'affaires a.i.

Source: United Nations Information System on the Question of Palestine (UNISQP), http://domino.un.org/unispal.nsf/, accessed on September 12, 2008.

Appendix 6

Jewish, Christian, and Muslim Prophecies

The religious prophecies that have been used to justify the founding of modern Israel are derived from biblical accounts, most notably verses 7-12 of Zechariah 10:

"And they of Ephraim shall be like a mighty man, and their heart shall rejoice as through wine: yea, their children shall see it, and be glad; their heart shall rejoice in the Lord. I will hiss for them, and gather them; for I have redeemed them: and they shall increase as they have increased. And I will sow them among the people: and they shall remember me in far countries; and they shall live with their children, and turn again. I will bring them again also out of the land of Egypt, and gather them out of Assyria; and I will bring them into the land of Gilead and Lebanon; and place shall not be found for them. And I will strengthen them in the Lord; and they shall walk up and down in his name, saith the Lord." (Zechariah 10:7-12).

The above verses cannot on their own be used as a justification for modern Israel, as they describe the return of the Israelites from Egypt to the Holy Land. Several interpretations have been offered in modern times to extend the implications of the above verses, including the following interpretation of verse 11 suggested by Adam Clarkes's commentary:

"I will bring them again also out of the land of Egypt - Here is an allusion to the passage of the Red Sea, on their coming out of Egypt, and to their crossing Jordan, when they went into the promised land; the waves or waters of both were dried up, thrown from side to side, till all the people passed safely through. When they shall return from the various countries in which they now sojourn, God will work, if necessary, similar miracles to those which he formerly worked for their forefathers; and the people shall be glad to let them go, however much they may be profited by their operations in the state. Those that oppose, as Assyria and Egypt formerly did, shall be brought down, and their sceptre broken."

It is not clear how "bringing them again out of the land of Egypt," can be understood to read "When they shall return from the various countries in which they now sojourn, God will work, if necessary, similar miracles to those which he formerly worked for their forefathers," but this is the type of interpretation that has been used to justify displacing Arabs from Palestine in favor of Jews.

The Qur'an does make reference to two triumphs of the followers of Moses followed by two defeats, as the following verses of Surah Isra indicate:

"And We ordained to the Children of Israel in the Book, that twice would you do mischief on the earth and be elated with mighty arrogance! When the first of the warnings came to pass, We sent against you mighty warriors of Our servants. They entered the very innermost parts of your homes; and it was a promise (completely) fulfilled. Then did We grant you the Return as against them: We gave you increase in resources and sons, and made you the more numerous in man-power. If you did well, you did well for yourselves; if you did evil, (you did it) against yourselves. So when the second of the promises came to pass, (We permitted your enemies) to disfigure your faces, and to enter your Temple as they had entered it before, and to visit with destruction all that fell into their power. If ye did well, ye did well for yourselves; if ye did evil, (ye did it) against yourselves. It may be that your Lord may (yet) show Mercy unto you; but if you revert (to your sins) We shall revert (to our punishments): and We have made Hell a prison for those who reject (all Faith). Verily this Quran does guide to that which is most right (or stable), and gives the glad tidings to the believers who work deeds of righteousness, that they shall have a magnificent reward." (Isra 17:4-9)

Early commentators of the Qur'an argued that the verses describe past events, while some contemporary commentators interpret the second triumph and defeat as referring to the current struggle in Palestine.

Evidently, prophecies involve a great deal of interpretation and speculation. Relating them to a particular historical timeframe is, therefore, problematic.

Recommended Reading

Anna Baltzer, *Witness in Palestine: A Jewish American Woman in the Occupied Territories* (Paradigm Publishers 2007)

Jimmy Carter, *Palestine: Peace Not Apartheid* (Simon & Schuster 2007)

Norman G. Finkelstein, *Image and Reality of the Israel-Palestine Conflict* (W. W. Norton 2003)

Gregory Harms and Todd M. Ferry, *The Palestine-Israel Conflict: A Basic Introduction*, Second Edition (Pluto Press 2008)

Rashid Khalidi, *The Iron Cage: The Story of the Palestinian Struggle for Statehood* (Beacon Press 2007)

Rashid Khalidi, *Palestinian Identity* (Columbia University Press 1998)

Elizabeth Laird and Sonia Nimr, *A Little Piece of Ground* (Haymarket Books 2006)

John J. Mearsheimer (Author), Stephen M. Walt, *The Israel Lobby and U.S. Foreign Policy* (Farrar, Straus and Giroux 2007)

Saree Makdisi , *Palestine Inside Out: An Everyday Occupation* (W. W. Norton 2008)

Recommended Readings

Ilan Pappe , *The Ethnic Cleansing of Palestine* (Oneworld Publications 2007)

Ilan Pappe, *A History of Modern Palestine: One Land, Two Peoples* (Cambridge University Press 2006)

James Petras, *The Power of Israel in the United States* (Clarity Press, Inc. September 26, 2006)

Charles D. Smith, *Palestine and the Arab-Israeli Conflict: A History with Documents* (Bedford/St. Martin's 2006)

Edward W. Said, *The Question of Palestine* (Vintage 1992)

Joe Sacco and Edward Said, *Palestine* (Fantagraphics Books 2002)

Karl Sabbagh, *Palestine: A Personal History* (Grove Press 2007)

Glossary

Arab-Israeli Wars – In the sixty years since its inception, Israel initiated five of the six major wars it fought. Below is a list of these wars:

- 1948 War: Israel refers to this war as the War of Independence, while Palestinians calls it the Nakba (Catastrophe).
- 1956 War: Israel joined Britain and France in attacking Egypt after the latter nationalized the Suez Canal in 1956.
- 1967 War: Also known as the Six-day War. In this war, Israel carried out what it called a preemptive attack against Egypt, Jordan, and Syria, and captured Gaza and Sinai, the West Bank, and the Golan Heights.
- 1973 War: This was initiated by Egypt and Syria, and led to withdrawal of Israel from Sinai and parts of the Golan Heights. The war also led to the peace negotiations between Egypt and Israel that culminated in the Camp David Peace Accords.
- 1982 War: Israel invaded Lebanon and forced the Palestinian Liberation Organization out of Lebanon after laying siege on Beirut that lasted for six weeks.
- 2000 War: The Lebanese resistance forces, led by Hezbullah, intensified its attacks on the Israeli army and its South Lebanon Army ally, forcing them out of southern Lebanon.

Glossary

Balfour Declaration – an expression of intent made in 1917 by the British government to support the creation of "a national home for the Jewish people." The declaration was made in a letter sent by Arthur James Balfour, the British Foreign Secretary, to Lord Walter Rothschild, a leader of the British Jewish community.

Bill Clinton – The 42nd president of the United States of America (1993 -2000)

Camp David Peace Accords – Two agreements signed, on September 17, 1978 by Anwar Sadat, the president of Egypt, and Menachem Begin, the prime minister of Israel, following negotiations at Camp David in the State of Maryland. Jimmy Carter, president of the United States, mediated the negotiations. The Accords paved the way for the Israel-Egypt Peace Treaty of 1979 whereby the two countries agreed to recognize each other and to end the state of war that had existed between them, which led to Israel's withdrawal from The Sinai.

David Ben-Gurion – A Zionist leader and the first prime minister, as well as the first president, of Israel.

Diaspora – A Greek term that means "the scattered." It refers to the scattered Jews throughout the world after their expulsion from the Holy Land by the Romans in the 2nd Century. Most recently, the term has also been used in reference to Palestinians who have been forced to live outside Palestine since 1948.

Far Right – the term refers to individuals and groups associated with extreme conservative politics. Far right supporters are often strong advocates for forcibly intervening in society in order to protect or promote values that are viewed as traditional.

Gaza – A coastal strip of land along the Mediterranean Sea between Egypt and Israel. After a protracted war of resistance, the Israeli government unilaterally decided to withdraw from Gaza, but maintained an economic blockad over the area. It is home to 1.4 million Palestinians squeezed into a 7.5 by 25 mile area (12 by 41 kilometers).

Geneva Convention – Four treaties signed in 1949 in Geneva, Switzerland. The treaties set the standards for humanitarian treatment of non-combatants and prisoners of war.

George W. Bush – The 43rd president of the United States of America (2001 -2008)

Hamas – A Palestinian group that takes its name from its Arabic acronym which means "Islamic Resistance Movement in Palestine." It was organized in 1987 by Sheikh Ahmed Yassin as the Gaza wing of the Muslim Brotherhood at the beginning of the First Intifada. Hamas was designated as a terrorist organization by the United States government in 1995. It won the first free elections in the Palestinian territories in 2006, and formed the government of the Palestinian Authority. The United States and its European allies refused to recognize the Hamas government, which continues to govern Gaza.

Hezbullah – Also spelled Hezbollah, is one of two major political parties that represent the Shiites in Lebanon. It holds 14 of the 128 seats in the Lebanese Parliament. It led the Lebanese resistance movement against Israel for two decades, and forced it in 2000 to abandon its bid to create a security zone in southern Lebanon that began in 1982. Hezbullah is officially listed as a terrorist organization by six countries: the United States, the United Kingdom, Israel, Canada, the Netherlands, and Australia. It enjoys popular support as a legitimate resistance movement in most of the Arab and Muslim countries.

International Law – The term refers to a set of agreements that binds together nation-states to uphold universally recognized values and standards.

Israelites – Refers to the children of the Prophet Israel or Jacob, particularly after they grew into large tribes in Egypt. They were led out of Egypt by Moses and eventually succeeded in establishing the Kingdoms of Israel and Judah.

League of Nations – The predecessor of the United Nations; it was founded as a result of the Treaty of Versailles in 1919–1920.

Likud Party – An Israeli political party that represents the major conservative political block in Israel.

Mahmoud Abbas – A Palestinian activist and member of the Palestine Liberation Organization (PLO). He served as an advisor to Yasser Arafat and played a crucial role in the Oslo agreement between the PLO and Israel. He was elected in 2005 president of the Palestinian Authority to replace Arafat. He has been locked in power struggle with Hamas since 2006.

Nakba – An Arabic term which means "Catastrophe," and often used by Arabs and Palestinians in reference to the creation of Israel

Neoconservatives – A group of liberals who switched parties during the Vietnam War and became Republicans committed to affirming America's global role and power. They believe in using America's military advantage to assert its role as the sole superpower.

The Occupied Territories – A term refers to the West Bank and Gaza which Israel occupied in 1967.

Oslo Agreement – the first direct, face-to-face agreement between Israel and the Palestinians. It led to the recognition of Israel by the PLO and paved the way for Peace Process negotiations that lasted from 1993 to 2000.

Palestinian Authority – an administrative organization established by the Oslo agreement to govern parts of the West Bank and Gaza

The Quartet – The Quartet on the Middle East, also known as the Diplomatic Quartet, Madrid Quartet, or simply the Quartet, is a group of nations and international and supranational organizations involved in mediating the Middle East peace process. The Quartet consists of the United States, Russia, the European Union, and the United Nations.

Glossary

United Nations Organization – An organizations of nation-states established in 1945 to replace the League of Nations.

West Bank – a landlocked territory on the west bank of the Jordan River that was occupied by Israel in 1967.

World Zionist Organization – umbrella organization for the Zionist movement, founded in 1897 in Basel, Switzerland, with the aim to create the Jewish State of Israel in Palestine.

Zionism – A political ideology and movement that calls for establishing a Jewish homeland in Palestine.

INDEX

About the Author

Louay Safi is a recognized authority on Islam and the Middle East. He published extensively on such issues as socio-political development, modernization, democracy, human rights, and Islam and the West. He is the author of ten books and numerous papers, including *Tensions and Transitions in the Muslim World* (University Press of America, 2003). His most recent books are *The Qur'anic Narrative* published by Praeger in 2008 and *Leading with Compassion*, published by Outskirts Press in 2009.

Dr. Safi is a frequent speaker on issues of leadership, human rights, democracy, Islam and modernity, world peace, and the Middle East. He appeared on numerous radio and TV programs, including CNN, BBC, Fox News, PBS, Middle East TV (MBC), Al-Jazeera TV, and Voice of America.